SPECTRUM®
EARLY YEARS

Basic Beginnings
FOLLOWING DIRECTIONS

Published by Spectrum®
an imprint of Carson-Dellosa Publishing LLC
Greensboro, NC

Spectrum
An imprint of Carson-Dellosa Publishing, LLC
P.O. Box 35665
Greensboro, NC 27425-5665

carsondellosa.com

ISBN 978-1-60996-889-2   01-044127784

Table of Contents

Welcome to *Basic Beginnings*

Basic Beginnings is a creative and developmentally appropriate series designed to fuel your child's learning potential. The early years of your child's life are bursting with cognitive and physical development. Therefore, it is essential to prepare your child for the basic skills and fine motor skills that are emphasized in the 21st century classroom. Basic skills include concepts such as recognizing letters, numbers, colors, shapes, and identifying same, different, and sequences of events. Fine motor skills are movements produced by small muscles or muscle groups, such as the precise hand movements required to write, cut, glue, and color. A child in preschool spends a lot of his or her day developing these muscles.

Basic Beginnings approaches learning through a developmentally appropriate process—ensuring your child is building the best foundation possible for preschool. Each activity is unique and fun, and stimulates your child's fine motor skills, hand-eye coordination, and ability to follow directions. Help your child complete the activities in this book. Each activity includes simple, step-by-step instructions. Provide your child with pencils, crayons, scissors, and glue for the various and creative activities he or she is about to discover.

Each book also includes three cutout mini books that reinforce the concepts your child is learning. You and your child will enjoy reading these simple stories together. Your child can make each story his or her own by coloring it, cutting it out, and, with your help, stapling the story together. Allow him or her to share the stories with you and others. Your child will begin to recognize sight words, hear vowel sounds, and understand sequences of events as he or she shares these delightful stories. With *Basic Beginnings*, the learning is never confined to the pages!

Introduction to *Following Directions*

Developing basic skills knowledge and fine motor control are important steps toward school readiness for your child; however, your child's ability to follow directions and his or her listening skills should not be overlooked. Learning how to listen and discern what is heard are essential skills for everyday living. Your child's cognitive development is rapidly growing and he or she can increasingly handle one, two, three, and four step directions. *Following Directions* builds the best foundation possible for gradually introducing multiple step directions. By allowing your child to be creatively expressive while completing these activities, he or she will have fun and retain better understanding of the basic following direction skills being reinforced in the activities.

Each activity includes simple directions for your child. Carefully read the directions one step at a time. As your child gains more visual and auditory memory control, you can try reading your child two directions at once to challenge his or her memory. For instance, begin by saying, "Color the flower red," and wait for your child to finish coloring. Then, tell your child, "Color the bee yellow." As your child improves, you may try saying, "Color the flower red and the bee yellow." This enhances your child's ability to recall and follow two step directions—which he or she will frequently encounter in the 21st century classroom. If your child exhibits any difficulty with visual or auditory memory skills, try some of the fun activities below before your child attempts any of the activities in this workbook.

What Does Not Belong?

Ask your child to listen very carefully as you tell a familiar story. Change or mix up some very important details, such as the "Three Little Pigs," who built a house made from straw, sticks, and construction paper; or, "The Three Bears" and the boy named Goldhat, who snuck into the bears' home and ate all the scrambled eggs. Tell your child to jump up and down whenever he or she hears something that does not belong in the original version.

Can You Do It?

Ask your child to do three things. Your child will listen to all three things before performing the tasks. For instance, ask your child to 1. Stand up. 2. Jump two times. 3. Touch his or her toes. If three tasks are too much for your child, start with two tasks. For variation, let your child give you three tasks to do!

Picture This

Show your child a photograph. Let him or her study it for 20 to 30 seconds. Put the photo down and ask your child to describe what he or she saw. Ask your child questions such as, "What color was the car in the picture? How many people were in the picture?"

Developmental Checklist

Between Ages of Two and Three:

- ☐ Imitates circular scribble and horizontal and vertical lines
- ☐ Builds a tower of 6 blocks
- ☐ Holds crayon with thumb and fingers (not fist)
- ☐ Snips with scissors
- ☐ Puts tiny objects in small containers
- ☐ Folds paper in half
- ☐ Pulls toys with strings
- ☐ Strings 1 to 4 large beads
- ☐ Uses a spoon
- ☐ Turns single pages of a book
- ☐ One hand begins to be dominant
- ☐ Paints with some wrist action
- ☐ Pounds, rolls, pulls, and squeezes play dough

Between Ages of Three and Four:

- ☐ Builds a tower of 9 blocks
- ☐ Snips with scissors
- ☐ Completes a 5–6 piece puzzle
- ☐ Holds a crayon with three fingers
- ☐ Copies a circle
- ☐ Copies vertical and horizontal lines
- ☐ Draws a person with a head
- ☐ Uses a spoon and fork with little spillage
- ☐ Opens rotating door handles
- ☐ Strings ½ inch beads
- ☐ Traces a square
- ☐ Unzips separating zipper; zips and unzips non-separating zipper
- ☐ Unbuttons large and small buttons
- ☐ Identifies body parts

Between Ages of Four and Five:

- ☐ Builds a tower of 10 blocks
- ☐ Strings ¼ inch beads
- ☐ Scissor skills improved – cuts on lines and cuts simple shapes

- ☐ Copies a cross and a square
- ☐ Can independently button and unbutton
- ☐ Uses dominant hand with better coordination
- ☐ Able to do 6–10 piece puzzles
- ☐ Can print some uppercase letters
- ☐ Draws a person with 2 to 4 body parts
- ☐ Holds writing tools with three fingers – control increasing
- ☐ Dresses and undresses independently – managing buttons and zippers
- ☐ No longer switches hands in the middle of an activity
- ☐ Builds a 6 block pyramid

Between Ages of Five and Six:

- ☐ Bounces and catches balls
- ☐ Builds a tower of 12 blocks
- ☐ Can build 3 steps from 6 blocks
- ☐ Draws angles, triangles, and other geometric shapes
- ☐ Draws a complete person with a head, body, legs, arms, and a face
- ☐ Can color within lines
- ☐ Cutting skills improved – can cut along lines and can cut out a circle
- ☐ Holds a knife in the dominant hand
- ☐ Copies first name
- ☐ Has mastered an adult grasp of a pencil
- ☐ Hand dominance is well-established
- ☐ Can use glue appropriately
- ☐ Prints numerals 1 to 5
- ☐ Enjoys working with a variety of mediums: paint, clay, glitter, chalk, glue, etc.
- ☐ Begins to tie shoes
- ☐ Can "sew" lacing cards
- ☐ Completes a 12–15 piece puzzle
- ☐ Learning how to print upper- and lowercase letters

Count and Color

Directions: Color **2** pencils.

Directions: Color **3** boxes of paint.

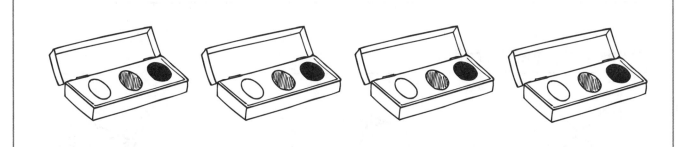

Directions: Color **4** paintbrushes.

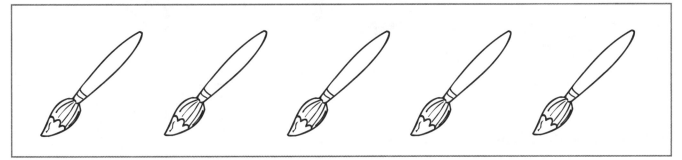

Directions: Color **5** boxes of crayons.

Following Directions

Count and Color

Directions: Color the bear **brown**.

Directions: Color the kite **red**.

Directions: Color the umbrella orange.

Color the Clown

Directions: Follow the directions below. Then, color the rest of the picture any way you like.

I. Color the stripes on the clown's hat **blue** and **green**.

Jumping Frogs

Directions: Follow the directions below. Then, color the rest of the picture any way
you like.

1. Color the frog on the rock **green**.
2. Color the frog on the lily pad **brown**.

10

I Am Special

Directions: Follow the directions below. Then, color the rest of the picture any way you like.

1. Draw your face.
2. Draw a picture on your shirt.

Fun on the Farm

Directions: Follow the directions below. Then, color the rest of the picture any way you like.

1. Color the duck in the pond yellow.
2. Color the barn **red**.

Let's Fly a Kite

Directions: Cut out the kites and follow the directions below. Then, glue the rest of the picture any way you like.

1. Glue the kite with hearts to the girl with long hair.
2. Glue the kite with dots to the boy with a hat.

Following Directions

Pet Fish

Directions: Cut out the fish and follow the directions below. Then, glue the rest of the picture any way you like.

1. Glue the fish with dots over the treasure chest.
2. Glue the long fish next to the starfish.
3. Glue the **purple** and **green** fish at the top of the water.

15

Animals in the Forest

Directions: Follow the directions below. Then, color the rest of the picture any way
you like.

1. Draw an orange circle around the squirrel in the tree.
2. Draw a red snake under the log.
3. Color two small trees green.

17

The Library

Directions: Follow the directions below. Then, color the rest of the picture any way
you like.

1. Color the bookworm **green**.
2. Put a **blue X** on the globe.
3. On the top shelf, color **3** of the standing books **purple**.

18

Who can zip?

Who can tie?

Who Can?

They all can zip.

6

Who can go out to play?

8

Notes to Parents

Directions: First, ask your child to color the mini book. Then, help him or her cut along the dotted lines. Next, have your child arrange the pages in the correct order. Staple the pages together. Read the story out loud to your child.

Extension ideas:
1. Ask your child to count each child in the story. Then, ask your child to count each teacher.
2. Have your child circle the word **they** every time he or she sees it.
3. Ask your child if he or she can zip his or her coat. Then, let your child show you.
4. Provide your child with shoes and laces. Let your child practice lacing shoes.

5

They all can tie!

7

They all can!

Insects in the Garden

Directions: Follow the directions below. Then, color the rest of the picture any way you like.

1. Color the flower with the bee on it yellow.
2. Color the butterfly **red**.
3. Draw a **blue X** on the flower in the top row without a bug on it.

Following Directions

Match the Same

Directions: Name each animal. Draw a line to match the animals that are the same.

What is Different?

Directions: Draw an **X** on the picture that is different in each row.

Who's the Same Size?

Directions: Follow the directions below. Then, color the rest of the picture any way you like.

1. Color the smaller horse **brown**.
2. Draw carrots for the two bigger rabbits.
3. Color the smaller frog **green**.

26

Largest to Smallest Dogs

Directions: Cut out the dogs below. Then, follow the directions.

1. Draw a collar on the largest dog.
2. Draw a **blue** hat on the smallest dog.
3. On a separate sheet of paper, glue the dogs in order from largest to smallest.

27

Smallest to Largest Trees

Directions: Cut out the trees below. Then, follow the directions.

1. Draw a **brown** monkey on the largest tree.
2. Draw an **orange** bird on the smallest tree.
3. On a separate sheet of paper, glue the trees in order from smallest to largest.

Following Directions

Matching Mittens

Directions: Draw lines to connect the matching mittens.

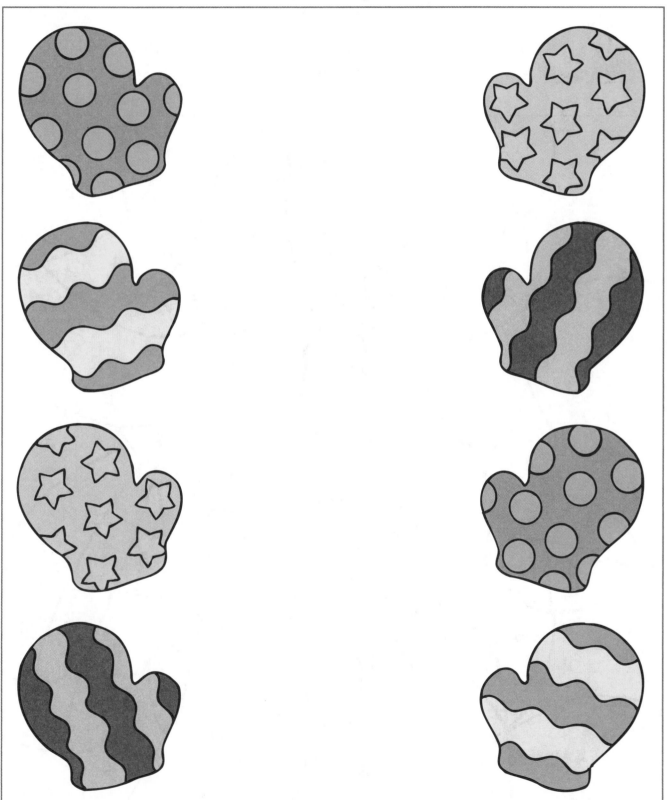

Who Is Hiding?

Directions: Look at the color key. Color each section the correct color.

1=yellow   3=orange   5=green

2=red   4=blue

Following Directions

What Is Hiding?

Directions: Look at the color key. Color each section the correct color.

B=brown   P=purple   Y=yellow
G=green   O=orange   R=red

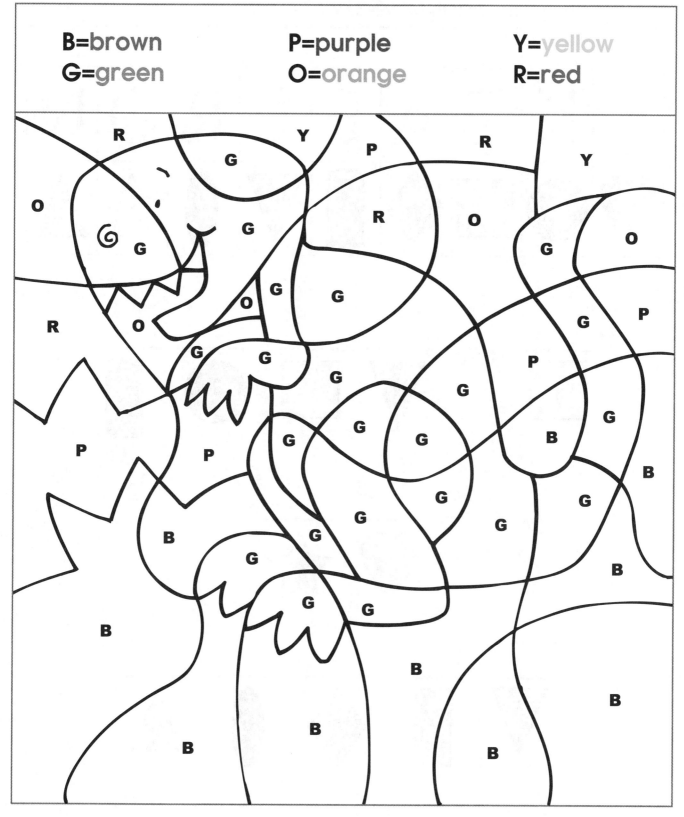

33

Secret Code

Directions: Look at each shape. Write the matching letter on the line above the shape. What does the secret sentence say?

Following Directions

What's Wrong at Home?

Directions: Some things look wrong in the house! Follow the directions below. Then, color the rest of the picture any way you like.

1. Look at the bedroom. Color the wrong object **red**.
2. Find the dog. Circle what is wrong.
3. Look at the bathroom. Color **2** wrong things **blue**.
4. Draw an **X** on **3** wrong things in the living room.

Draw a Pig

Directions: Follow the steps to draw a pig.

Porky Little Pigs

Pass the peas, please.

Pass the pancakes, please.

Pass the potatoes, please.

6

Pass the popcorn, please.

8

Notes to Parents

Directions: First, ask your child to color the mini book. Then, help him or her cut along the dotted lines. Next, have your child arrange the pages in the correct order. Staple the pages together. Read the story out loud to your child.

Extension ideas:

1. Ask your child to oink like a pig every time he or she sees the letter **Pp** in the story.

2. Have your child circle each uppercase **P** with a **purple** crayon. Then, circle each lowercase **p** with a **pink** crayon.

3. Make pancakes together. Explain each step to your child to show the importance of following directions in order.

5

Pass the pizza, please.

7

Pass the pillows, please.

Following Directions

Draw a Lion

Directions: Follow the steps to draw a lion.

Draw a Fox

Directions: Follow the steps to draw a fox.

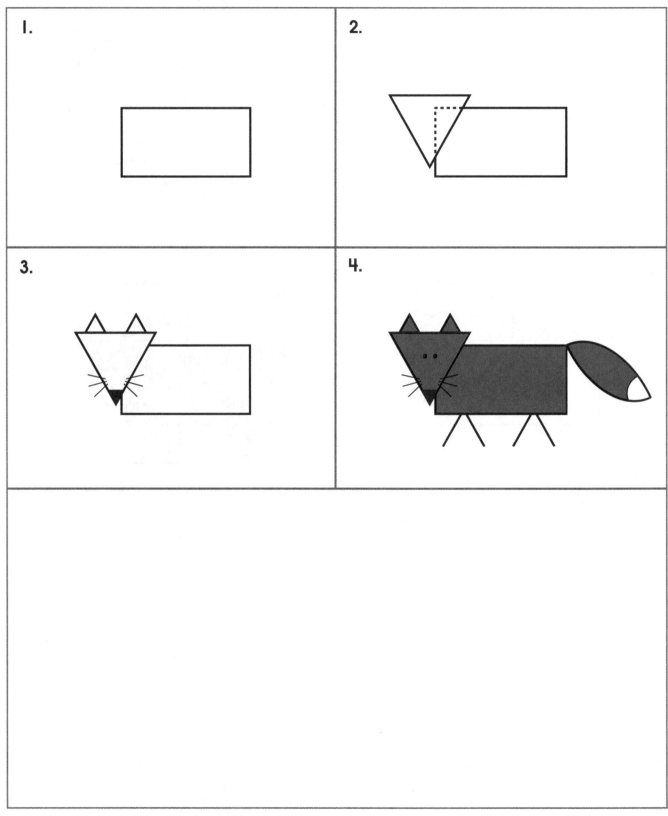

Where Do the Toys Belong?

Directions: Cut out the toys and follow the directions below. Then, color the rest of the picture any way you like.

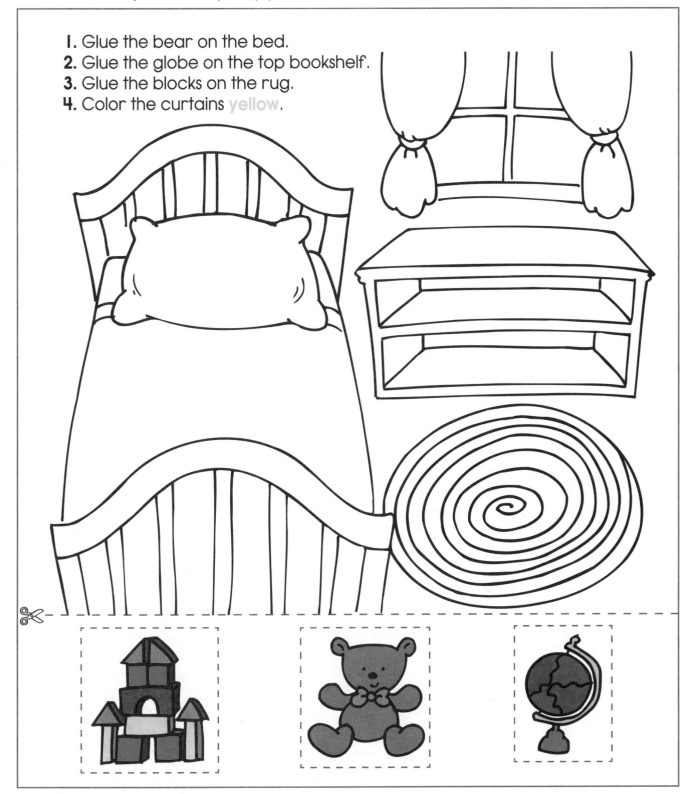

1. Glue the bear on the bed.
2. Glue the globe on the top bookshelf.
3. Glue the blocks on the rug.
4. Color the curtains yellow.

Following Directions

The Tree

Directions: Cut out the pictures and follow the directions below.

1. Glue the bee over the tree.
2. Glue the squirrel under the tree.
3. Glue the owl up in the tree.
4. Glue the sun in the sky.

45

School Tools

Directions: Cut out the supplies and follow the directions below.

1. Glue the crayons on the front pocket.
2. Glue the pencil and paper on the backpack.
3. Glue the scissors next to the backpack.
4. Color the backpack your favorite color.

Following Directions

Sequencing Puzzle: Penguin

Directions: Cut along the dashed lines. Glue each piece in the correct order. Color the penguin.

49

Snowman Puzzle

Directions: Cut out the pieces and follow the directions below.

1. On a separate sheet of paper, glue the circles in the shape of a snowman.
2. Glue the hat on top of its head.
3. Glue the sticks where the arms should be.
4. Draw a face on the snowman.

Finished snowman

Where Are My Friends?

Directions: There are **7** animals hiding in the picture. Find and circle each animal.

raccoon	bird	deer	squirrel
owl	rabbit	bear	

Where Are My Toys?

Directions: There are **7** toys hiding in the picture. Find and circle each toy.

wagon	kite	paints	sailboat
teddy bear	ball	truck	

2

Find the sock.

4

Find the shoe.

1

Look
and
Find

3

The sock is in the box.

Following Directions

6

Find the shirt.

8

Notes to Parents

Directions: First, ask your child to color the mini book. Then, help him or her cut along the dotted lines. Next, have your child arrange the pages in the correct order. Staple the pages together. Read the story out loud to your child.

Extension ideas:
1. Ask your child to draw more hiding objects in the story.
2. Have your child circle the word **find** every time he or she sees it.
3. Play hide and seek together. Give your child directions on how to play. Then, hide several objects in a room. Encourage your child to find each object.

5

The shoe is in the box.

7

The shirt is on me.

Following Directions

Search and Find: Rr

Directions: Find and color the things that start with the letter **Rr**.

59

Search and Find: Cc

Directions: Find and color the things that start with the letter **Cc**.

60   *Following Directions*

Search and Find: Ss

Directions: Find and color the things that start with the letter **Ss**.

Following Directions

Search and Find: The Playroom

Directions: Look at the objects below. Find and color them in the picture. Then, color the rest of the picture any way you like.

Following Directions

Search and Find: My Backyard

Directions: Look at the objects below. Find and color them in the picture. Then, color the rest of the picture any way you like.

63

Search and Find: Sailing

Directions: Look at the objects below. Find and color them in the picture. Then, color the rest of the picture any way you like.

64